# Advance Praise for
# To All the Magic in Me

"*To All the Magic in Me* is a cosmic exploration through the human spirit. Pavita Singh takes us on a journey through dark, hidden emotions to brilliant, light-filled ones. This poetry collection is a soul cleanse and serves as a profound and powerful nod to the inner workings of our hearts."

—Elizabeth Buechele | Founder, The Smile Project

"In a world that often encourages absolutes, this honest and vulnerable collection teaches readers to enjoy the ugly complexities without judgement. We are good. We are bad. We are silly. We are burdened. We are insecure. We are vain. We are real people. Thank you, Pavita, for capturing and applauding our humanness."

—Marney A. White, PhD, MS |
Clinical Psychologist | Faculty, Yale University

"Pavita Singh's book really spoke to me and was easy to relate to. I felt like I was reading love letters to myself that I had written myself. It is amazing finding people similar to you who have similar experiences. It is a sweet reminder that we are not all so diff          ------te after all. It

D1506702

also reminded me of pieces of myself here and there that I have lost sight of and am finding again. I highly recommend reading Pavita's book. You might find or remember a piece of yourself in there."

—Zayda Renna | Reiki Master | Author, *Spill the Light*

"As I read Pavita Singh's *To All the Magic in Me*, I could not help but be reminded of a child blowing on a dandelion pappus—each billowy seed going in a different direction. 'To Loneliness,' 'To Amusement,' 'To Jealousy,' 'To Wisdom'—each bringing us to disparate parts of the poet's imagination and allowing us to visit for as long as we have a mind to."

—Billy Manas | Author, *Kickass Recovery: From Your First Year Clean to the Life of Your Dreams*

To All the Magic in Me

# A COLLECTION OF LOVE LETTERS
# TO ALL OF LIFE'S EMOTIONS

## PAVITA SINGH, MPH

publish
y⬚ur gift

TO ALL THE MAGIC IN ME
Copyright © 2021 Pavita Singh
All rights reserved.

Published by Publish Your Gift®
An imprint of Purposely Created Publishing Group, LLC

Printed in the United States of America
ISBN: 978-1-64484-381-9 (print)
ISBN: 978-1-64484-382-6 (ebook)

A portion of the proceeds from *To All the Magic in Me* will benefit Girls Health Ed, a nonprofit organization whose mission is to advance gender equality by fostering healthy, informed, and empowered decision-making in adolescent girls and young women ages 8 and older, particularly those from underserved communities in the United States and internationally, through medically accurate, gender-transformative, and intersectional comprehensive health and sexuality education. Learn more at girlshealthed.org.

*To the Universe.*

*To my loved ones.*

*To the important people and events in my life that have in some way, shape, or form made me who I am and played a role in the fruition of this collection.*

*To all the magic in me.*

*Thank you.*

# Table of Contents

Introduction ....................................................... 1

To Amusement .................................................. 9

To Boredom ...................................................... 11

To Inspiration .................................................... 13

To Frustration ................................................... 14

To Creativity ..................................................... 16

To Loneliness ................................................... 18

To Solitude ....................................................... 19

To Sensuality ................................................... 21

To Lust ............................................................. 23

To Jealousy ...................................................... 25

To Ignorance .................................................... 27

To Intelligence ................................................. 29

To Wisdom ....................................................... 30

To Honesty ....................................................... 31

To Mystery ....................................................... 32

To Hypocrisy .................................................... 34

To Fear ............................................................. 36

To Courage ....................................................... 38

To Surrender .................................................... 39

To Ambition ..................................................... 41

To Laziness ...................................................... 42

To Debt ............................................................... 44

To Envy ............................................................... 46

To Abundance ..................................................... 48

To Guilt .............................................................. 50

To Forgiveness ................................................... 52

To Exhaustion .................................................... 53

To Health ........................................................... 55

To Respect .......................................................... 56

To Insecurity ...................................................... 57

To Confidence ..................................................... 59

To Presence ........................................................ 60

To Addiction ....................................................... 62

To Stress ............................................................. 65

To Balance .......................................................... 67

To Restlessness ................................................... 68

To Patience ......................................................... 70

To Perfectionism ................................................ 72

To Passion .......................................................... 74

To Failure ........................................................... 75

To Empowerment ............................................... 76

To Stubbornness ................................................. 78

To Growth ........................................................... 79

To Depression ..................................................... 81

To Sadness .......................................................... 83

To Bliss ............................................................... 84

To Optimism ............................................... 86

To Empathy ............................................... 87

To Apathy ................................................ 88

To Youth.................................................. 90

To Aging ................................................. 92

To Grief.................................................. 94

To Nostalgia ............................................. 95

To Embarrassment ......................................... 96

To Irritation............................................ 98

To Anxiety ............................................... 100

To Relief................................................ 103

To Peace ................................................. 104

To Appreciation .......................................... 106

To Imagination........................................... 108

To All the Magic in Me ................................... 109

About the Author ......................................... 111

# Introduction

"We fall in love with people's flaws. The perfect person would be impossible to love," writes poet and author J. Strelou. Life is anything but flawless. It is filled with stains and blemishes. Along with moments of calm are moments of stress and turmoil, sometimes even in the same day. Pleasure is frequently accompanied by pain. And therein lies life's beauty.

Humans are inherently complex creatures rife with contradictions. These clashing contradictions, seemingly unaesthetic on the surface, come together to create something incredible—the experience of being alive. Within us is a multitude of emotions, ranging from equanimity to excitement, loneliness to connection, repulsion to desire, and everything in between and beyond. People often go through life doing whatever they can to avoid negative emotions. I'll be the first to admit that sometimes I do this as well.

For a large proportion of my life, I have struggled with anxiety. In spite of my struggles, I had always been known for the most part to exhibit a positive demeanor. In the beginning of 2016, however, I was hit with a life-changing event. The details of this event are perhaps the topic of another book. What I will share, however, is that I was angry. Surely I had

had encounters with anger before this incident, but now, anger was at the forefront of my psyche and a very real part of my day-to-day existence. At the time, I was taking part in an apprenticeship with an online publication called *elephant journal*, and one of my assignments was to write and submit a poem. I used this assignment as a coping exercise and published a poem called "Dear Anger."

"Dear Anger" was a letter of gratitude to the emotion of anger—an appreciation of its necessity at that point in my life and of the lessons it had to teach me. It was a first step in getting better. Writing this poem was one of my first realizations that negative emotions do not have to be avoided like the plague. "Dear Anger" was soon followed by an article entitled "Why I will Not Apologize for Complaining," in which I acknowledged that while complaining may not be productive all the time, it does, in fact, feel good. On social media and in our everyday lives, we are often inundated with positive, feel-good quotes and "good vibes only" messages. I actually find "good vibes only" to be quite a harmful philosophy. These types of messages, well intentioned as they might be, often contribute to people burying their negative feelings and faking positivity, which can then lead to other types of pathologies—either physical or mental—in the long term. As I wrote in "Why I will Not Apologize for Complaining," the act of complaining is a recognition of the not so bright side of life, and when it is complemented with gratitude for the things that *are* going well, it can actually serve to facilitate healing.

A year and a half later, my sister, Gunita, graduated from Georgetown Law and came home to California, where our family was living at the time, to study for the bar exam—arguably the hardest academic exam there is. I lived with Gunita for a month during her first semester of law school. It was the first time in my life I had ever seen her anxious. As I quickly learned, law school will do that to a person. Our whole lives, I was used to being the anxious sibling, and to now see my sister in this unpleasant state with which I was so intimately familiar was extremely difficult for me. In her remaining two years of law school, her anxiety tapered. It came back and multiplied in scale that grueling summer she prepared to take the nation's most difficult bar exam. At one point during the summer, Gunita had a conversation with someone who encouraged her to sit with her anxiety—to listen to what it was trying to tell her before she gracefully released it as an emotion that no longer served her. This was a transformative experience for my sister, as it offered her a new perspective on coping with anxiety. Although I was only a witness in this situation, it was transformative for me too. Having studied mental health treatment in college and graduate school, I was so used to articles and lectures that demonstrated the efficacy and effectiveness of replacing negative thoughts with positive thoughts as a means of improving one's mood and addressing such conditions as anxiety and depression. Hearing about this conversation my sister had had reaffirmed what I had earlier learned about the important role that negative emotions play in our lives and reminded me that they need not be shunned, but rather embraced. This new perspective has since been helpful for me as I have coped with my own anxiety. And in case you were wondering, Gunita passed the California Bar on her first attempt. She is now starting her third year as a successful attorney, and I couldn't be prouder.

Fast forward yet another year and a half. At the end of 2018, I was going through a serious bout of depression, feeling lost and unclear about my purpose in life. One morning, Gunita, who was staying with me in my new home in New York City during the winter holidays, took me into my bathroom and stood in front of the mirror with me. She told me to say positive affirmations to myself in the mirror. She said a few to get me started and asked me to repeat after her. "I am beautiful." "I am smart." "I am a good person." "I love myself." With effort, I repeated each affirmation as I was told. "Now you come up with some of your own," she said.

There was a pause. "I am enough," I said through the tears, remembering that my friend Inna had made me set a picture of the saying as my iPhone background a week earlier, just before I left California. "I am enough" written in green letters on a pink background (one of my favorite color combinations) has been my iPhone Lock Screen background ever since December 15, 2018.

"More," she said.

I paused again. "I hate this exercise!" I vehemently responded. Both of us left the bathroom feeling frustrated and defeated and went to separate rooms to cool off.

The truth is that I did not actually hate that exercise. In fact, starting in the new year a little over a week later, I made it a point to at least try to say positive affirmations daily, either out loud in the bathroom mirror or by writing them down in my journal. What made me make that comment, however, was that when I was feeling as low as I did, trying to come up with positive affirmations was an onerous task. It felt fake. Sometimes I feel the same way about gratitude journaling, which my coaches encourage me to do daily.

None of this is to say that people should not practice saying positive affirmations or do gratitude journaling. They are both helpful practices that I often do and that I recommend as some of many tools people can use for self-care. I include positive affirmations as an exercise when teaching self-esteem workshops to girls and young women as part of my work with my nonprofit, Girls Health Ed. Since October 2020, I have also taken part in the Smile Project Ambassador Program, an initiative by an organization called The Smile Project that challenges ambassadors to find at least one small thing each day that brings them even the tiniest bit of joy and share it on social media. I do this almost every day on Instagram and thoroughly enjoy it.

All of this being said, to exclusively say positive affirmations or to recognize only the good things going on in one's life is to deny half of what it means to be human—having negative emotions. I believe that as long as they are dealt with in a healthy manner, negative emotions should be invited and felt just as much as positive emotions. What you are about to read, in my opinion, is a much richer and much more authentic depiction of the human spirit than positive affirmations or gratitude for what is going well—love letters to the whole range of life's emotions, both positive and negative.

The list of emotions portrayed in this collection of poems is not by any means comprehensive. The poems are not displayed in any particular order. Some of the poems are juxtaposed with ones about their opposite emotions, but others are not. Given the complexity of human emotions, not every emotion has an exact opposite. Furthermore, as these poems illustrate, not every negative emotion is 100 percent negative, and not every positive emotion is 100 percent positive—there are positives within the negatives and negatives within the positives. If anything in the works that follow, or even in this introduction, appears contradictory, perhaps it is. That is the point. To be a human is essentially to be a living contradiction. We all have within us multiple aspects of our identity that do not always mesh. Navigating these incongruities is messy, confusing, and outright frustrating. But it is also beautiful, enlightening, and magical. And if anything you read in this collection seems repetitive, it might be. As different as each of our emotions are, they are all interrelated, and each emotion entails attributes of several others. Finally, even though I have written about the 61 emotions or states of being in this collection, I am not claiming that I know how to successfully deal with all of them. It is a lifelong process that I am constantly figuring out.

As John Legend sings in one of my favorite songs, *All of Me*, "Love your curves and all your edges, all your perfect imperfections." With the poems in this collection, my message to you is similar: learn to fall in love with all of your emotions, for they are all part of you. Perhaps try having conversations with these emotions, as I have done in the letters you are about to read. Even if it doesn't always feel good, I encourage you to embrace these emotions and see the light in all of them. Doing so will help you unleash all the magic in you.

# To Amusement

Dear Amusement~
Of all of my friends,
You are the clown of the group.
You don't let me take life,
Or myself, for that matter,
Too seriously.
"What fun is living
Without a daily dose of humor?"
You always say.
You've taught me that laughter
Is the richest nutrient,
And you never let me go a day
Without that nourishment,
Even when it's hard to do.
Whether reminding me of funny stories,
Or making me watch my favorite sitcoms,
Or getting me to spend a night out
With fun-loving company,
You always find a way
To make me laugh,
Sometimes so hard

That my sides hurt
And it's difficult to breathe—
Which, ironically,
Is one of the best feelings ever.
You show me lighthearted pleasure
In everyday occurrences
And allow me to embrace my playful side,
Which boosts my own mood
And sparks happiness
In those around me.
Thank you, Amusement.
Love, ~Me

# To Boredom

Dear Boredom~

You make me want to escape

Certain situations,

As you don't create

The most pleasant of surroundings.

But from you,

New ideas are born.

You give the mind permission

To wander,

As is its nature,

And it can go quite far

Without even leaving home.

You give me no choice

But to make do

In whatever confines

In which I'm stuck,

And from that,

Much magic can arise.

You also allow me
To simply be
And find comfort
In the blank spaces
In between.
Thank you, Boredom.
Love, ~Me

# To Inspiration

Dear Inspiration~

You drive me to create incredible things,

Build the life of my dreams,

And lead by example,

Motivating others to do the same.

You give me confidence in myself,

Reminding me how awesome I truly am—

A pillar to which others aspire.

Thank you, Inspiration.

Love, ~Me

## To Frustration

Dear Frustration~
Urghhhhh.
Rawrrrrrr.
Fuuuuuuck.
Sharp exhales
Accompanied by lip trills,
Other expletives,
And sometimes screams.
These are some of the noises you make
When you leave my body.

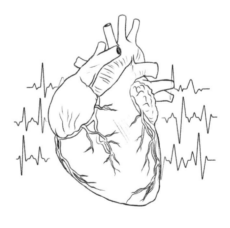

You exponentially increase my heart rate,

Drawing mountain ranges on an EKG.

You make me wonder

What is wrong with myself

And what is wrong with the world.

You make me question

Why we can't move faster,

Why we can't do better,

Making you one of the top drivers

Of change.

Of progress.

Thank you, Frustration.

Love, ~Me

# To Creativity

Dear Creativity~
You have ignited in me
Passionate curiosity.
You constantly expand
My ever-growing comfort zone
By making me try new activities,
Learn new skills,
And embrace new experiences.
With your guidance,
I ideate innovative solutions to problems
And bring beauty to the world
With my prolific productions
That you enable.
Through the act of making,
You let me forget about everything else
And simply connect with my soul.
Thank you, Creativity.
Love, ~Me

# To Loneliness

Dear Loneliness~

How I long

For a companion

Who understands

The enigmatic inner machinations

Of my mind.

How I pine

To not have to translate

The words my soul speaks

And risk losing their meaning.

How I wish

To share some of my burden

When I am in pain,

And to laugh together

At the extraordinary and the mundane.

You push me to leave my cocoon,

Open my eyes,

Put myself and my love into the world,

And attract what connections may arise.

Thank you, Loneliness.

Love, ~Me

# To Solitude

Dear Solitude~
You are the most
Comforting company,
For you ensure
That I'm true to me.
24/7, as long as I live,
I'm the only one
With whom I am.
You give me no choice
But to love that person.
Be my own best friend.
Because if not me,
Then who?
Who will love me
The way I do?
Together, Solitude,
We can do so much.
We can read.
Sleep.
Dream.

Breathe.

Be.

Some of the best ways

To spend the days.

Thank you, Solitude.

Love, ~Me

# To Sensuality

Dear Sensuality~

You have given me my body,

Which is uniquely mine,

And I love it.

You make me proud

Of all it can do.

You help me accept and appreciate

My scars and flaws,

For my physical imperfections

Are part of my beauty.

You remind me to nourish my body

With healthy food

And show it love

Through movement and touch.

You acutely tune me in

To all of my senses.

Sight.

Smell.

Sound.

Touch.

Taste.

You make me feel desirable
And give me permission
To give myself pleasure
In any way I wish
And express my connection to others
Through physical affection.
Thank you, Sensuality.
Love, ~Me

# To Lust

Dear Lust~
You make it so fun
To be alive.
In fact,
You are one of the reasons
I am even alive
In the first place.
I love how you bring out
My primal nature
And make me shiver
And my hairs rise
At the touch of another.
I relish at the way
You send pulsating vibrations
Through all my cells
Causing me to lose all control
When our bodies collide,
Inciting an internal explosion.
An exchange of energy.
A rush in dopamine.
Oxytocin.
Vasopressin.

An interaction so intense
That the stars
Stare from the sky
In awe.
Thank you, Lust.
Love, ~Me

# To Jealousy

Dear Jealousy~
You make me feel
That I'm the only person
In the world
Who should matter.
Because of you,
I need to be
Everybody's favorite—
The one person
To whom they turn,
As if love
Is a scarce resource
To be hoarded
And as if a compliment to another
Is an insult to me.
If anyone threatens
My position on top,
You drop me to the bottom,
Thinking that there's no space to share
And that there's no in between.
You do not seem to grasp

That there's no way I can be
Everything
To everybody,
No matter how amazing I am.
You do not understand
That love is the one entity
That when shared
Is not divided
But rather multiplied.
You see my importance and value,
But you inflate them unnecessarily.
Instead of making me bitter
When someone doesn't give me
The love or attention
To which you believe
I'm entitled,
Why not make me
Better?
Maybe you can invite me
To find my own love and attention
And give it
To myself.
Thank you, Jealousy.
Love, ~Me

# To Ignorance

Dear Ignorance~
No matter how much I learn,
No matter how much I know,
There will always be someone else
Who knows even more.
As hard as I may try,
You make it impossible
To find all the answers
I seek.
"Live the questions,"
You say.

You keep me humble,
Allowing me to rely on others
For knowledge and information.
You are my reminder
That learning is a lifelong,
Never-ending process.
You help me find comfort
In the uncertainty
Of not knowing
But simply trying.
Exploring.
Doing.
Living.
And letting the answers come
When they will come.
Thank you, Ignorance.
Love, ~Me

# To Intelligence

Dear Intelligence~
You make me excited about learning
And show me the lessons to be found
In all people, places, and things.
Because of you,
I am not afraid of challenges,
For you have given me
A rich library of resources
In which I am more than capable
Of finding the answers
Even to the toughest questions.
I show you love
With every puzzle I solve
By building and strengthening neural networks.
You've taught me that the things I know
Have value to the world.
That knowledge is power,
And with that power,
I can do so much good.
Thank you, Intelligence.
Love, ~Me

# To Wisdom

Dear Wisdom~

You and Intelligence

Make an interesting pair.

You guide me in appropriately

Applying my knowledge.

You encourage me to invite new experiences

And absorb the lessons from them.

You remind me to exercise good judgment

And help me to gracefully accept

The consequences of my actions.

Above all else,

You teach me to be

A good person.

Thank you, Wisdom.

Love, ~Me

# To Honesty

Dear Honesty~

You transparently show me my truth

And ensure that I honor it.

You make sure my words and actions

Align with my thoughts and feelings.

You give me the courage

To share my truth with others

Compassionately and respectfully.

Because of you,

I feel no need

To hide any part of me,

For I love every part of me.

With all my behaviors,

You help me earn the trust of others,

Ensuring that I can be depended upon.

Thank you, Honesty.

Love, ~Me

# To Mystery

Dear Mystery~

You know I am a complex being.

You see my many layers.

You cover them

Like a blanket,

Protecting me,

Knowing that I need not expose

All of me

All at once

To everyone.

You give me permission

To seduce.

To tease.

To slowly strip

Away the layers

At my own pace,

In my own space,

To those I deem worthy

Of my core.

Of my naked soul.

I reveal and re-veil
As I wish,
And you allow me to keep
Certain parts of me
All to myself,
Encouraging others to engage
Their imagination.
Thank you, Mystery.
Love, ~Me

# To Hypocrisy

Dear Hypocrisy~
Sometimes you get lazy,
Or maybe just confused,
And you don't always correctly match
My actions with my words.
I might do one thing,
Say another,
Say one thing,
Do another,
Not because I am dishonest,
But because I am human.
Imperfect.
Complex.
Evolving.
Real.
You remind me that life
Is not black and white.
Doing the right thing
Is not always easy.
It is a winding, twisted
Process.

Other emotions
Or life circumstances
Might get in my way.
Sometimes, that's okay.
Maybe not forever,
But for right now.
Nonetheless, you alert me
When my alignment is off,
When the puzzle pieces don't fit,
Getting me to try to do better
Next time.
Thank you, Hypocrisy.
Love, ~Me

# To Fear

Dear Fear~

To you, I am so dear

That your reason for being

Is to keep me safe.

You don't want to see me hurt,

And you will do anything

In your power

To prevent that.

You might not realize

That without pain,

There is no gain.

And without gain,

Things stay the same.

And in the long run,

That is a loss

Of which to be afraid.

So all I ask

Is for you to stay tame.

Thank you, Fear.

Love, ~Me

# To Courage

Dear Courage~

Life presents us with various challenges,

And sometimes I have tough choices to make.

Even if it's not easy,

You help me make them.

You give me the strength

To do what is right.

You do not let me

Shy away from obstacles.

Rather, you remind me

That I can handle

Anything that comes my way.

You help me persevere

And come out even stronger

Than I was before.

Thank you, Courage.

Love, ~Me

# To Surrender

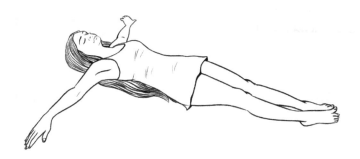

Dear Surrender~
Sometimes I feel the need
To control
Everything that happens to me.
You strip me
Of the illusion
That I can.
You remind me
That there's only so much
I can do
Before the Universe works its
Magic,
And with that comes
A certain sense of
Calm.

You constantly teach me
After all my hard work
To sit back
And simply
Trust.
Thank you, Surrender.
Love, ~Me

# To Ambition

Dear Ambition~
You see so much potential in me
And know how capable I am
Of achieving the best.
You help me reach great heights
And don't let me stop,
For there will always be more to do
In this lifetime
And those that follow.
No matter how tough the circumstances,
You remind me
That I'm several times tougher.
Because of you,
I never give up.
Thank you, Ambition.
Love, ~Me

# To Laziness

Dear Laziness~
You don't let me get
A whole lot done
For no other reason
Than just not wanting to.
You extinguish
The burning flame inside me,
Unplugging my power,
Turning me into
An object at rest
That wants to stay at rest,
At least for some time.
For many years,
I was conditioned to think otherwise,
But you have taught me
That this is okay.
"I don't feel like it,
At least not now,"
Is a perfectly valid excuse
According to you.
I could do nothing,
And I'd still be alive.

The things that I do
Do not define me.
My output is not my value.
Rather, the contents of my
Heart and soul
Are my essence.
Sometimes it is nice
To simply be.
That, too, is living.
So how could that not be
Productive?
Thank you, Laziness.
Love, ~Me

# To Debt

Dear Debt~

You are stressful company.

Sometimes you make it hard

To survive,

Making people worry

When and if

They'll even be able

To eat.

To sleep.

To learn.

But you also demonstrate

That just a little

Can indeed go a long way.

As much as people

Love to think otherwise,

You show us

That the world owes us

Nothing.

You don't let anyone get too greedy

Or live beyond their means.

Sometimes what we have

Is more than enough.

The need for excess
Is an illusion.
You are a reminder
Of the power of hard work
And that if we look
In the right places
We will always find
A reason
To say
"Thank you."
So for that,
Thank you, Debt.
Love, ~Me

# To Envy

Dear Envy~

Even though I have everything,

You love to make me think

That it's not enough.

Comparison is your favorite game.

You are conniving and manipulative,

Convincing me

That others' successes

Are my failures

And that their happiness

Is my sadness,

Even if just for a split second

Before the re-realization

That I am no less of a

Badass

Than anyone else

And am my own kind of beautiful.

That split second is enough

(A word you don't understand)

To eat at my psyche

And rob me

Of a moment of peace.

Nonetheless,

You motivate me

To get.

To achieve.

To be

All that I'm capable

Of being.

Just know

That I can also do that

Without you.

Thank you, Envy.

Love, ~Me

# To Abundance

Dear Abundance~

You are full of riches,

But beyond that,

You are generous.

You ensure that all of my needs are met,

And for that, I am eternally grateful.

You invite me to appreciate and enjoy

The fruits of my hard work.

We celebrate together,

And you are the life of the party.

You fill my plate

All the way to the edges,

Not only with necessities,

But also with the luxuries I desire.

You encourage me to share

What I have with others,

For I have more than enough.

The more I share,
The more I effortlessly attract what I want.
You are the magnet
For everything wonderful in my life.
Thank you, Abundance.
Love, ~Me

# To Guilt

Dear Guilt~
I know you all too well.
You make me feel regret
For the bad things I've done,
But also the burden
Of the things I have not.
You enter my space
And make me feel
The pain of others
As if it is my own,
Often at the expense
Of my own wellbeing.
It is a heavy load to carry,
And it stays with me,
Even when everyone else
Has long let go
Or forgotten.
While you help me learn
From my mistakes
And tune into others' emotions,
You take up too much room.

You are too much to bear.

Honestly, you do not have much value.

You have overstayed your welcome.

It's time to pack your baggage

And leave.

Thank you, Guilt.

Love, ~Me

# To Forgiveness

Dear Forgiveness~
I have met many people in my life,
Some of whom have done me wrong,
Some intentionally,
And others through no fault of their own.
You've helped me realize
That no one is perfect.
As much as I may want to
Or feel that I need to,
You don't let me be consumed
By my own mistakes
Or the mistakes of others,
Reminding me that they are not mine
To hold onto.
You rid me of all past hurts,
Not for anyone's peace of mind
But my own.
Thank you, Forgiveness.
Love, ~Me

# To Exhaustion

Dear Exhaustion~
You are at once
Glorified
And frowned upon.
But honestly,
I find you quite pleasant
And welcome you.
You force me to rest—
One of my favorite things to do—
And ensure that I get
A restorative slumber
And a fresh start.

You bring needed endings
And new beginnings.
You are an invited pause.
A reset button
That everyone needs.
You are the reminder
That we can't keep going
Without also stopping.
So please come
Anytime.
Thank you, Exhaustion.
Love, ~Me

# To Health

Dear Health~

I literally cannot survive without you.

You keep my body fully capable

Of doing everything it needs to do.

You give me ample energy

To function at maximum capacity.

Because of you,

I can do so much.

Dance.

Sing.

Run and frolic in the park.

Play with friends.

Work multiple jobs.

Hold a child.

Cuddle with a companion.

Live my best life.

You radiate vibrancy

Through every cell of my being.

It seeps through my skin

And reflects in my smile.

Thank you, Health.

Love, ~Me

# To Respect

Dear Respect~

I am a unique individual

With my own beliefs and emotions.

Nobody else is exactly like me,

And to you, that is beautiful.

You appreciate me for who I am.

Often, I have a lot to say,

But you restrain me from vocalizing

All my thoughts,

For even in moments of discord,

You ensure that I treat others

With dignity,

Just as I expect to be treated.

You allow me to harmoniously coexist with others,

Making sure I am good to everyone else,

And most importantly,

To myself.

Thank you, Respect.

Love, ~Me

# To Insecurity

Dear Insecurity~
A part of me is missing.
That's how you make me feel.
A sentiment so powerful,
It almost seems real.
What is it that's not there?
It's hard for you to say.
Whatever it is, Insecurity,
You ruin so many of my days.
You tell me all the ways
That I am not enough,
That whatever I do,
I just don't measure up.
You constantly pressure me
To keep on doing more,
Tricking me into thinking
That people are keeping score.
If I don't act my best,
You're the biggest reason why,
And you make it so hard to know
What's true and what's one of your lies.
Of all my states of being,

You're probably the least understood.
I don't know why you're here
Or what you think you're doing that's good.
Are you trying to keep me safe?
Stop me from getting hurt?
Win me other people's love?
Or just keep me on high alert?
I wish I knew what you were about
So I could try to be your friend,
Because it seems like part of you will linger
Until the very end.
There are few things I want more
Than to feel good about myself.
I just don't know if your misguided tactics
Are really what will help.
Thank you, Insecurity.
Love, ~Me

# To Confidence

Dear Confidence~

You are my biggest advocate.

When I look at myself in the mirror,

You tell me how incredible I am.

"You are smart and strong and beautiful.

You are everything good in the world,"

You say.

And I believe you.

You help me carry myself

With grace and poise

And attract the love and respect of others

Because of how you've taught me

To love and respect myself.

Because of you,

I am not afraid

To show off my positive qualities,

For you have shown me

That they make the world better.

Thank you, Confidence.

Love, ~Me

# To Presence

Dear Presence~

You and I

Have a difficult relationship.

You try to befriend me,

And I have trouble letting you in.

But when we do spend time together,

You keep me in the here and now,

Reminding me that the past is left behind,

And the future is yet to come.

This moment here
Is really all we have.
When I let you,
You help me enjoy it to the fullest,
Encouraging me to take in the experience
Using all of my senses,
Forcing me to appreciate
That this moment, too,
Is fleeting.
When my thoughts wander,
As they often do,
You are patient with me,
Bringing me back
To the only thing that's true,
Which is this moment here and now—
This moment that is a gift.
Thank you for the present.
Thank you, Presence.
Love, ~Me

# To Addiction

Dear Addiction~

How attractive you seem

On the surface,

Drawing me in towards

Objects and activities

That are fun.

You pull me in so deep,

That there's nothing else I see.

So focused you keep me,

But at what cost?

Minutes become hours.

Hours become a day.

Before I know it,

So much time is lost.

Time I'll never get back.

What a high price to pay.

I've forgotten to eat.

Didn't get any sleep.

Barely made any progress on work.

Neglected all my household chores.

Maybe it's better to stay away
Or at least limit
What distracts me
From doing what I need to do
To achieve my goals.
But you make it nearly impossible
To say no,
The way you keep bringing me back
For just a little bit more
With your allure so great,
Convincing me that I'm incomplete
Without the spice of my vices.

The way you make me jitter
When they're missing
And simultaneously make me numb
As if life has lost its excitement.
This cycle repeats
Until your "just a little more"
Leaves me poor.
Addiction, you certainly keep me engaged,
But your consequences have shown me
The importance of
Boundaries.
Thank you, Addiction.
Love, ~Me

# To Stress

Dear Stress~
You are a deep river
Into which I drown.
I slowly sink to the bottom,
Straining to return to the surface,
Struggling to catch
A breath of fresh air.
But still, you make me fight
And keep on swimming
In order to survive.

I come out cold.

Drenched.

Tired.

Lost.

Perhaps this is your reminder

To start at the shallow side

And not dive straight

Into the deep end—

Fun or necessary as it may seem—

And tackle more than I can handle

At a time.

Thank you, Stress.

Love, ~Me

# To Balance

Dear Balance~
Thanks to you,
I live a well-rounded life.
You allow me
To hold many responsibilities,
Adding spice to the quotidian.
You help me prioritize
And effortlessly flow
Through different aspects of my being,
Giving due attention to each of them,
While also ensuring that
I care for myself
And bring the best me
To everything I do.
Thank you, Balance.
Love, ~Me

# To Restlessness

Dear Restlessness~
My mind is a garden
With ideas as seeds.
And you are the unnatural
Hormones in the soil
Causing rapid sowing,
Uncontrollable growing
Of unhealthy weeds
Spoiling my flowers.
My mind is an object in motion
That wants to stay in motion.
Not only do you keep it moving,
You turn it into a
Tornado.
Why don't you instead
Try nourishing it
With calming sounds?
Positive thoughts?

Encouraging words?
Why don't you give it an opportunity
To take a break
And continue working
Continue producing
Continue sowing
Healthy seeds
Just a little bit later?
Thank you, Restlessness.
Love, ~Me

# To Patience

Dear Patience~

Sometimes we fight,

But you help me trust

In the timing of the Universe.

You have taught me

That life is a process

Where some things come quickly,

And others more slowly.

"What's the rush?" you ask.

Like your friend Presence,

You remind me

That there's nowhere else to be

But right here,

Right now.

From you, I have learned

That there is beauty in waiting.

"If you rush,

You might miss out," you say.

That's why the scenic route

Is often the long one.

When I'm hard on myself,

You stop me,

Assuring me that I'm doing my best,
Even when I forget.
Thank you, Patience.
Love, ~Me

# To Perfectionism

Dear Perfectionism~

You are simultaneously

My best friend

And my worst enemy.

You're like an authoritarian parent.

My own parents

Are not authoritarian.

So why are you?

You know my potential,

Which is extremely high,

And you make me go for it.

You see no barriers.

Absolutely none.

But you don't let me have any

Fun!

Where's the enjoyment

In anything we do?

I will do everything you want me to

And more.

So why don't you just chill
And let me fall in love
With the process
Instead of the product?
Thank you, Perfectionism.
Love, ~Me

# To Passion

Dear Passion~

Oh, how I love you.

You make me love what I do

And engage with enthusiasm.

You light a fire in me,

Helping me stay energized and motivated,

Propelling me to become

Better and better.

You fill me with pleasure

And keep me immersed

In what I'm doing

In a state of blissful flow

And pure enjoyment.

Few things feel better than this.

Thank you, Passion.

Love, ~Me

# To Failure

Dear Failure~

You are underappreciated,

But I'll tell you,

You are awesome.

You always keep it interesting,

Getting me to try new things,

And identify what works and what does not,

The latter list likely containing a lot.

You show me where things might have gone wrong,

Not letting me stay hard on myself for too long,

Snapping me out of it, keeping me plugging along.

Getting better and better with each attempt

Is never a waste—it is time well spent.

You always present an opportunity to learn,

And that's the investment with the greatest return.

Thank you, Failure.

Love, ~Me

# To Empowerment

Dear Empowerment~

You let me do anything

To which I set my spirit.

Once you set my wheels in motion,

There's nothing stopping me.

I hear you say,

"You are smart.

You are capable."

You are right.

You put my deepest desires within reach

And help me manifest them.

But that's not all.

You see my magnificence,

And with it,

You help me lift others up with me.

Together, we celebrate them

As we would ourselves,

Knowing there is room for us all

At the top.

You see our brilliance,

And you give us each a crown.

As long as we wear it,

Nothing can bring us down.

Thank you, Empowerment.

Love, ~Me

# To Stubbornness

Dear Stubbornness~
You are comfortable.
You make it feel safe
To hang onto you.
You keep me firmly rooted,
Steadfast in my beliefs,
Set in my routines.
You usually find a way
To get me what I want,
And I love you for that.
But what will happen
When life throws curveballs
Or changes?
That is yet to be figured out.
Thank you, Stubbornness.
Love, ~Me

# To Growth

Dear Growth~

I am terrified of you.

Often, I hate you.

Like a nagging parent,

You say you know

What's best for me.

I don't want to admit it,

But sometimes

You're right.

The world is always changing,

And you make me change with it.

It hurts.

You are a sadist

Taking pleasure in my pain.

But you often produce
Astonishing results,
Like coal becoming a diamond,
Or a caterpillar
Becoming a chrysalis
Becoming a butterfly.
You force me to constantly learn and evolve,
To become even slightly better
Than I was yesterday.
But you work in strange ways,
Because sometime getting better
Means getting worse,
And getting worse
Means getting better.
You always demand more of me,
Like I'm your slave.
I am your canvas,
Your work in progress,
Never reaching perfection,
Yet somehow always enough.
Thank you, Growth.
Love, ~Me

# To Depression

Dear Depression~
My darkest times in life
Have been spent with you.
Time and time again,
I survive.
You make it painfully difficult
To get out of bed.
To eat.
To laugh.
To sleep.

To enjoy the things I do.
To even get through
The hours of the day.
I despise the way
You famish my soul,
Starving me
Of energy and motivation,
Leaving me unsure
Of what I'm doing in this world
Or where to go
For sustenance.
Yet somehow,
I always manage
To trudge through your quicksand,
Knowing that in the worst of times,
When I'm stuck at the bottom,
The only place to go
Is up.
Knowing that I can look back
And say,
"I'm alive."
Thank you, Depression.
Love, ~Me

# To Sadness

Dear Sadness~
People don't like you.
They avoid you,
Thinking you are unpleasant.
Uncomfortable.
But I embrace you.
You bring to the surface
Buried emotions
Begging to be released,
And with you
Come tears.
To cry
Feels almost as good
As to laugh.
You are a catharsis.
A cleansing.
Thank you, Sadness.
Love, ~Me

# To Bliss

Dear Bliss~

You make me so happy.

There are periods where we meet

With great frequency,

And other times, our visits

Are fewer and farther between.

But when we are together,

All is right with the world.

You make the colors shine brighter

And the air taste sweeter.

I feel my tummy tumble

When you are around

And can flit through the air

With levity.

You make me feel liveliness

In my muscles, nerves, and bones

And fall in love

With everything around me.

In your presence,

Excitement and calm coexist,

And I can't help but smile.

Laugh.
Maybe dance a little.
Together we bask
In the glory of the day,
Making it
The best of our lives.
No matter how long or brief,
These are the moments
For which I live.
Oh, how I hope
We meet more often.
Seeing you is a gift
I don't want to miss.
Thank you, Bliss.
Love, ~Me

# To Optimism

Dear Optimism~
If there is a reason
For waking up in the morning,
You are it.
No matter how bad things get,
You are the hope
That they will get better.
That is motivation enough
To keep going.
In any situation,
No matter how loud
The naysayers may dissuade,
You block out their noise.
You are the first to consider
The best-case scenario.
And when others bring up
The worst-case scenario,
You are our reminder
That it's still not that bad
Because no matter how terrible it gets,
It will always get better.
Thank you, Optimism.
Love, ~Me

# To Empathy

Dear Empathy~
I don't always like
How you make me feel
But you make me
A better person.
You connect me to others,
Allowing me to walk
A few steps in their shoes
And see the world
Through their eyes.
It is because of you
That I feel compelled
To help
When I witness distress.
You bring tears to my eyes
When I see another cry.
Because of you,
I do what I can
To make it
Just a little bit better.
Thank you, Empathy.
Love, ~Me

# To Apathy

Dear Apathy~

You are not too interesting.

When you are around,

Nothing really matters.

You turn me into a

Robot,

Aimlessly

Going through the motions

Without a care.

You are neutral,

Which is sometimes needed

When riding life's rollercoaster

Of extremes.

Perhaps your best quality

Is that you keep me

Detached.

Thank you, Apathy.

Love, ~Me

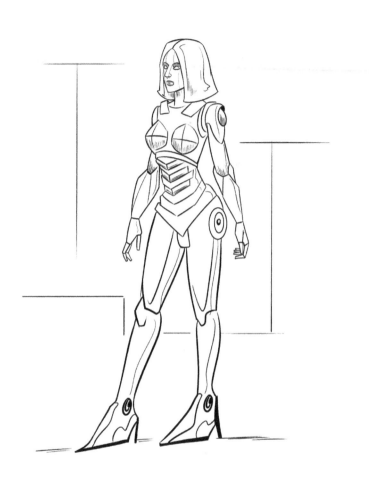

# To Youth

Dear Youth~
As many years
As I've been alive,
You stay with me.
You fill me with energy
And help me see the world
With a beginner's mind
As if every day
Is my first day.
You haven't been tainted
By the realities of the world.
To you, anything is possible.
You see nothing but opportunity
And have so much excitement
About life that's yet to be lived.
You embrace and encourage
My innocence.
My childlike quirks.
You make me look and feel
Beautiful.

I know
That you'll always be
Part of me
Through all the years.
Thank you, Youth.
Love, ~Me

# To Aging

Dear Aging~

Many people are afraid of you.

Including me.

With you,

Naivety

Is no longer an excuse,

And you make my accomplishments feel

Less significant.

You are said to bring wisdom.

But in many ways,

You supposedly make life

Even harder

Than it already is.

But in what position am I

To say?

You will find your home

In the circles under my eyes,

In the creases of my skin,

In the sprouts of silver

Among the lush fields of black

On my scalp.

You will permeate my internal organs

And make yourself comfortable.
You're already decreasing
My "bullshit tolerance."
Maybe you'll bring me closer
To those I love.
Perhaps you will help me
Fall even more in love
With me.
I feel as though
We're on the cusp of meeting.
You're slowly making
Your first subtle hints of appearance
In my youthful body,
But you've always been part of my
Soul.
Let's see what else you bring.
Thank you, Aging.
Love, ~Me

# To Grief

Dear Grief~
I don't know you that well,
But you teach us
That our time is brief.
That nothing truly belongs to us.
You release us from attachment.
It is hard to accept,
But you show us our own strength
And how much love we have.
You help us cherish old memories
And build new connections.
You remind us that we are all energy,
And energy never dies—
Only changes.
You show us that there is peace
In returning to our first home—
The eternal source.
Thank you, Grief.
Love, ~Me

# To Nostalgia

Dear Nostalgia~
You are a reminder
Of the richness of life.
Of all experiences had
And memories made.
To reminisce
Is exhilarating
And builds anticipation
Of what is still to come.
Thank you, Nostalgia.
Love, ~Me

# To Embarrassment

Dear Embarrassment~
I am only human
Just like everyone else.
As long as I'm alive,
I will always make mistakes,
Do things of which I'm not proud,
And harp over what I could've done
Differently,
Perhaps better.
You are one of my
Harshest critics,
The way you burn my skin
And cause profuse sweating,
Making me cringe
And want to bury my head
Into the rest of my body
And just disappear
For a little while
Even though no one else
Is thinking about
Or even remembers
What happened.

But you're also a reminder
Of the lightness of life.
If I take myself too seriously,
You stop me,
Giving me permission
To make fun of myself,
To laugh at myself,
Allowing others
To laugh with me.
Thank you, Embarrassment.
Love, ~Me

# To Irritation

Dear Irritation~

Sometimes there are moments in the day

Where I just do not feel okay.

Something as innocuous

As the buzz of my phone

Or someone asking

A simple question

Can feel like the most

Unbearable

Thing in the world.

You bring all my attention

To what's bothering me.

In these moments,

Nothing lifts my mood.

And heck,

I don't even care.

You let me know

In that time

That that's fine.

Instead of calming myself,

I would rather

Lash out.

Snap.

Swear.

Fight.

Not because I mean it

Or because that's who I am,

But simply because

For a split second

That's what satisfies me.

When this happens,

You allow me

To give myself a break.

To forgive myself

As others forgive me.

You remind me that I'm

Human

And give me a chance to feel

Less than perfect.

Thank you, Irritation.

Love, ~Me

# To Anxiety

Dear Anxiety~

What a relationship we have.

Over the decades,

I've filed some restraining orders

Against you.

Klonopin.

Prozac.

Ativan.

Xanax.

Zoloft.

Ashwagandha.

Reiki.

Meditation.

Kirtan.

Yoga.

Therapy.

Love.

What can I say?

Sometimes you are necessary

In order for me to perform.

You give me drive,
And sometimes work to keep me alive.
But like me,
You can be
Intense and stubborn.
You break me down and
Wake me up from my sleep
With pain in my chest,
Heaviness in my gut,
And throbbing in my temples.
You make me struggle to breathe and
Anticipate the worst.

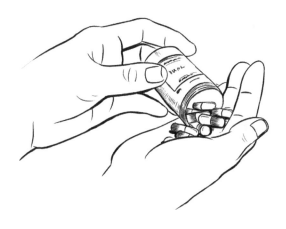

When you are around, I am
Easily irritated by all stimuli
And ready to scream and cry.
But I am tougher than you,
And I force myself
To make it through.
You are a terrifying,
Most troublesome feeling.
I can't always control
When you come and go.
But you usually teach me something
When you're here.
Decades with you
Has given me no option
But to learn to cope
With your presence.
I can't say I like you much,
But you're part of my story,
And you're part of my strength.
So for that,
Thank you, Anxiety.
Love, ~Me

# To Relief

Dear Relief~
You lift the heavy weights I carry
Off my shoulders.
You bring a glimmer of light
To the dark clouds.
You give me permission
To exhale
The breath I've been holding.
With that, I feel lighter.
My chest feels cleaner,
No longer clogged
With toxic waste.
You remove barriers,
Making it so much easier
To move along.
Thank you, Relief.
Love, ~Me

# To Peace

Dear Peace~
We need more of you
In the world,
And I need more of you
In my life.
To spend just a minute with you
Is a blessing.
When you are around,
My deep inhales and exhales
Imitate the ebbs and flows
Of the ocean waves.
It is a moment in which
I am free of worry
And everyone gets along.
You create a mosaic
Of diverse pieces,
Coming together
To make something even richer

Even more beautiful
Than the sum of its parts.
A true work of art.
Thank you, Peace.
Love, ~Me

# To Appreciation

Dear Appreciation~

I often get out of bed

With pain in my chest and head,

Dreading having to do

All that I need to.

Inundated with feelings of stress,

I might think my life is a bit of a mess.

But as I get up and go about my day,

You make me see all the little things that do go my way.

Like a plate of delicious food,

Which can uplift my mood,

Finishing a work project and saying "the end,"

Or all the time I spend with friends.

Moving my body in dance and fitness,

The pretty sights I get to witness,

Being able to take a long nap,

Receiving a gift in the mail to unwrap.

Experiencing even a minute of serenity

Is something I cherish—truly the best amenity.

Before I sleep, you make me write all this down,
Which has the power to make a smile from a frown.
So even if I wake up feeling sad,
You're my reminder that it's not so bad.
Thank you, Appreciation.
Love, ~Me

# To Imagination

Dear Imagination~
You create space
For incredible ideas
To inhabit my mind.
You've built in it
A beautiful playground
Where you watch my thoughts run wild,
Allowing me to envision
A better and brighter future
For myself and all beings.
With you by my side,
Nothing is out of reach.
You give me the power
To make my dreams a reality.
To put pen on paper
And share
All the magic in me.
Thank you, Imagination.
Love, ~Me

# To All the Magic in Me

Dear Me~

You are flawed.

You are perfection.

You are a flawed perfection.

You are a treasure chest of emotions—

Rough and messy,

Clashing and contrasting,

Often contradictory,

But all part of you.

All authentic.

And all beautiful.

Within you, you have all the power,

The Universe's blessings,

To do absolutely anything—

Your personal toolkit

To navigate this crazy, complex world.

To spark your inner light

And keep it glowing bright.

Be yourself.

Love yourself.

Embrace your brilliant, glorious chaos,
For that is genuine,
That is real.
That is your perfection,
And that is your magic.
To all the magic in me,
Thank you.
Love, ~Me

# About the Author

Pavita Singh is a polymath whose mission is to spread light, love, learning, and laughter and leave some sparkle wherever she goes. Her interests include mental health, education, youth empowerment, gender equality, languages, and creative arts. Pavita is the Executive Director of Girls Health Ed, the Director of Content & Communications at Konversai, and a Project Manager and Editor at Publish Your Gift. She also has her own editing business called pavEDITa. Her writings have been featured in *HuffPost*, *elephant journal*, and *Medium*.

Pavita studied at Yale University, where she received her Master of Public Health in Social & Behavioral Sciences, and New York University, where she received her Bachelor of Arts in Gender & Sexuality Studies, Linguistics, and Child & Adolescent Mental Health. She revels in creation, exploration, movement, connection, relaxation, wandering, laughter, and time with family and friends. Pavita has been to 38 countries and 25 US states and lives in New York City. *To All the Magic in Me* is her first published book.

Connect with Pavita on Instagram @power.pav.girl or visit her website, pavitasingh.com

## CREATING DISTINCTIVE BOOKS
## WITH INTENTIONAL RESULTS

We're a collaborative group of creative masterminds
with a mission to produce high-quality books to position
you for monumental success in the marketplace.

Our professional team of writers, editors, designers,
and marketing strategists work closely together to ensure
that every detail of your book is a clear representation
of the message in your writing.

**Want to know more?**
Write to us at info@publishyourgift.com
or call (888) 949-6228

Discover great books, exclusive offers, and more at
**www.PublishYourGift.com**

Connect with us on social media

@publishyourgift

CPSIA information can be obtained
at www.ICGtesting.com
Printed in the USA
BVHW031703101122
651683BV00021B/340

9 781644 843819